be happy.

Published in Richmond, Virginia by Give More Media.
ISBN: 978 0 615 23180 8

(804) 762-4500
GiveMore.com/Smile

smile&move™

it's all about attitude and action™

for all of us

contents

the story

MY DAUGHTER AND NIECE OPENED their lemonade stand at the front of our neighborhood.

Lemonade stands were everywhere that weekend. All were raising money for cancer research; it was a community service effort, part of a city-wide program.

Sitting at a distance, watching the girls work as cars pulled over to patronize their stand, I noticed what seemed to be a less than positive and energetic approach to serving their customers. It reminded me of the adults that I've encountered in too many places, who seemed put out or moved with complete indifference.

In a lull between visitors I asked, "Why are you doing this lemonade stand, girls?"

"To get our community service hours for school," they said.

"Any other reasons?"

"To raise money for cancer."

"Right," I said to their pre-teen eye roll. "Can you think of anything else?"

Silence.

"Anything?"

"Dad, please."

This was a core value issue – one worth the effort and challenge. "These people are stopping to be served lemonade because they might be thirsty but also so they can help *you* help people with cancer. They're your customers and they have places to go but they're giving you their support, their time, and money.

You need to approach them happily, with a smile. And then you need to move quickly to get them their drink so they can enjoy it and move on.

You're not doing them a favor. They're doing you a favor. They don't have to buy the lemonade and they don't have to buy it from you. You need to smile and move, girls.

SMILE AND MOVE."

we smile by...

being awake

being awake

ATTENTIVE. ENGAGED. INTERESTED.

It's caring about those with whom we connect and serve, having concern for what they need and want, and listening to not only what's said, but to the true message implied. It's asking questions about how we can help.

smile & move fact...

Watching is an important part of listening. Over 50% of a message's meaning is communicated through body language... and another 38% is conveyed through the speaker's tone. We've got to listen to more than just the words.

"Messages: The Communication Skills Book," by M. McKay, M. Davis and P. Fanning (1995).

And when we give our focused attention to the situations and people around us, everyone benefits.

Research shows that people who have high-quality connections enjoy mental and physical health benefits including lower stress, lower blood pressure, and better immune system functioning.

High-quality connections also help people feel better at work... helping them to be more creative and resourceful, and to learn new skills faster.

BE AWAKE.
(Researchers call it "conveying presence.")

smile & move idea...

To make better connections with people (and learn much more), when you're talking with someone be sure to allow a small gap of silence between what they say... and your response.

This will help people know you're truly listening.

(Remember: a breath is not **always** taken at the end of a sentence or thought.)

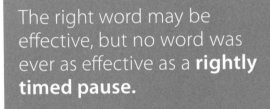

The right word may be effective, but no word was ever as effective as a **rightly timed pause.**

Mark Twain (1835–1910)
Novelist and humorist

we smile by...

being thankful

being thankful 🎁

SO MANY OF US ARE lucky in some way. Some, even more so. Occasionally, we'll have moments that remind us of our luck.

The positive moments…

- Our work is recognized as meaningful by a colleague, manager, or customer.
- A good friend or family member calls and brightens our day, reminding us of the wonderful people in our lives.
- We're finally able to buy that special thing we've always wanted.

The tough moments…

- We'll see someone who appears less fortunate, or hear of a friend losing a job.
- We'll see someone working in a job that seems physically difficult, or learn of a friend's or colleague's new illness.

We're reminded, but…

A little time goes by. A few distractions play out. A couple of things get in the way of the easy, and we find ourselves back to less than thankful (perhaps even complaining… again).

smile & move idea…

Ever caught yourself beginning a sentence with "Knowing my luck…" and concluding with something negative?

For many of us (even you), perhaps it should be "Knowing my luck, I'll win the lottery."

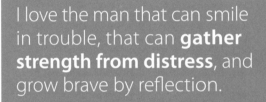

I love the man that can smile in trouble, that can **gather strength from distress**, and grow brave by reflection.

Thomas Paine (1737-1809)
Political theorist and writer

We need to more consistently approach our days and work with gratitude and remember that we're not entitled to either – that they're gifts.

And the most powerful way to express our gratitude is by serving others as well as we possibly can, to put their needs before our own (in whatever role we're in).

To be unable to work, to serve, and to have meaning to others… that is truly unfortunate, unlucky.

We should **BE MORE THANKFUL** for the opportunities we're given.

---

smile & move fact…

Research shows that people who are encouraged to express gratitude report feeling happier, more excited and joyful, and even have fewer headaches and colds.

"Counting blessings versus burdens: Experimental studies of gratitude and subjective well-being in daily life," by R.A. Emmons and M.E. McCulluogh (2003).

we smile by…

being approachable

being approachable

WE ALL HAVE OUR "CUSTOMERS." And most of us have more than one customer group.

- A teacher serves his students as well as his school administrators (and perhaps even parents).
- An administrator serves her teachers in addition to a group of county administrators.
- A doctor serves his patients as well as his practice partners and perhaps a hospital staff.
- A CEO serves her stockholders as well as her management team and outside clients.

It's an interdependent world.

We depend on each other and as a result, we need to make ourselves accessible and approachable to our people (customers, constituents, colleagues, patients, leaders). We're not islands and can't expect to succeed on any significant level without connecting with people.

Being approachable is being receptive to occasional interruptions, making ourselves regularly accessible to others, and doing it with a smile... a smile not only with our mouths and eyes but an internal and authentic smile that can be felt by those with whom we interact.

If we create a situation where people feel the need to walk on eggshells when they come to us (asking for help, guidance, or a solution), eventually they'll stop walking on eggshells and go to someone else. If that happens, whether we're a leader or a follower, our value to others is gone. And when we're shopping for something and the store no longer provides the value we're looking for, what happens? We go somewhere else.

BE APPROACHABLE.

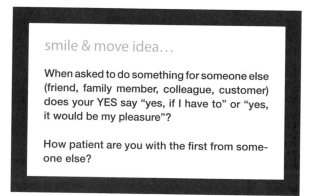

smile & move idea...

When asked to do something for someone else (friend, family member, colleague, customer) does your YES say "yes, if I have to" or "yes, it would be my pleasure"?

How patient are you with the first from someone else?

However fragmented the world, however intense the national rivalries, it is an inexorable fact that we **become more interdependent** every day.

Jacques Cousteau (1910-1997)
French marine explorer

I love the quote, but the word inexorable isn't really approachable, is it? So... inexorable means inevitable.

Consciously or unconsciously, every one of us does render some service… If we cultivate the habit of doing this service deliberately, our **desire for service** will steadily grow stronger, and will make, not only our own happiness, but that of the world at large.

Mahatma Gandhi (1869-1948)
Indian leader and activist

we smile by...

complaining less ⊘

complaining less

BE CAREFUL TO KEEP YOUR personal challenges to yourself and those closest to you.

The people around you have challenges of their own and likely won't be able to give yours real attention. Also, in time (if we're awake), we begin to see what a complete waste of energy a complaint (or whine) is even to the people who might be most interested... ourselves.

Once we embrace this fact, complaining less should be fairly easy... until someone around us begins. At that point, we might have a tendency to join in. When we smile, we remember to do what we can to minimize this tendency. When we move, we express care for another's situation and help if we can.

STRIVE TO BE COMPLAINLESS.

smile & move fact…

To feel good and flourish, researchers say that people need a 3:1 positivity ratio. That means they need to hear three positive statements for every complaint.

Having a positive attitude has been linked to mind-body-spirit benefits including:

- Greater creativity and increased intuition
- Better cardiovascular health and reduced risk of stroke
- Increased resilience and happiness

"Positive Affect and the Complex Dynamics of Human Flourishing," by B. Fredrickson and M.F. Losada (2005).

Relatively speaking, many of us who complain about anything really shouldn't.

When the complaints begin among our circle of people, maybe we should be the ones who throw out the idea that many people struggle with far more real (and basic) challenges than we do.

That's when we might hear...

"Well, it's all relative."

And when we hear that, we should remember (and maybe remind each other) that we're all human beings and relatively speaking, most of us with a roof over our heads, food in our stomachs, and work to contribute are living every day…

Relatively wonderfully.

This is the **true joy in life**, the being used for a purpose recognized by yourself as a mighty one; the being thoroughly worn out before you are thrown on the scrap heap; the being a force of Nature instead of a feverish selfish little clod of ailments and grievances complaining that the world will not devote itself to making you happy.

George Bernard Shaw (1856–1950)
Irish playwright and critic

we smile by…

smiling, really 👄

smiling, really 👄

PLEASANT PEOPLE ARE MORE ENJOYABLE than those who aren't.

- Working with them is better.
- Buying from them is better.
- Selling to them is better.
- Playing with them is better.

And pleasantness begins with a smile.

smile: smī(-ə)l

1: a facial expression in which the eyes brighten and the corners of the mouth curve slightly upward…
2: a pleasant or encouraging appearance

With all of its benefits, it should be easier to make smiling the rule rather than the exception.

Ideas to help make smiling a habit in your world…

1. Create a few positive mental anchors – a visual of your child or spouse, a pet, a joke, or a hilarious moment. Give each image a name and write it down. If time allows, pause and reflect on one **just before** you make contact with someone.

2. Place a mirror labeled with the word "smile" on your desk or in a common area. Use it to remind and check yourself throughout the day, or before you make a call or talk with someone.

3. Post or carry actual pictures that make you smile. Change them periodically so their effect remains fresh. Make one the background on your computer.

4. Get a friend or coworker to help by smiling at you (beaming, really) when they see you frowning. It will serve as a silent but effective reminder of what you're trying to accomplish.

5. Just before you make contact with someone, imagine you're about to see an old friend you haven't seen in a long time… remember how lucky you really are.

6. Watch how others begin to reflect and return your smile (encouraging you to smile even more).

ARE YOU SMILING YET?

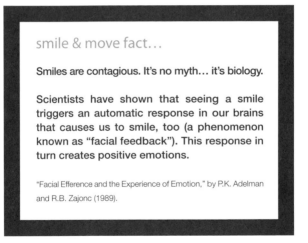

smile & move fact…

Smiles are contagious. It's no myth… it's biology.

Scientists have shown that seeing a smile triggers an automatic response in our brains that causes us to smile, too (a phenomenon known as "facial feedback"). This response in turn creates positive emotions.

"Facial Efference and the Experience of Emotion," by P.K. Adelman and R.B. Zajonc (1989).

we move by...

starting early
& going long

starting early
& going long

THINK ABOUT YOUR SCHEDULE.

Starting or leaving on time — whether it's at work, at a meeting, or at an event — is what's expected.

And if we do only what's expected, we can be fairly sure we'll rarely enjoy any special result.

A couple of quick questions…

- Of the 20 or so days you work each month, how many times do you start earlier than is expected of you?
- How many times do you work longer hours than are required?

To start early and go long sends a message of purpose, commitment, and respect — to others and yourself — and assures better results over time. To be even one minute late, or rarely be challenged ending your day on time, sends a completely different message.

Get lost in your service to others.

GIVE MORE AND YOU'LL ENJOY MORE.

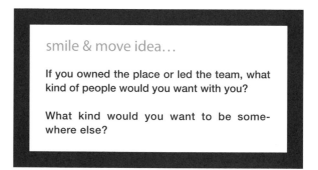

smile & move idea...

If you owned the place or led the team, what kind of people would you want with you?

What kind would you want to be some-where else?

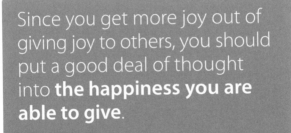

Since you get more joy out of giving joy to others, you should put a good deal of thought into **the happiness you are able to give**.

Eleanor Roosevelt (1884–1962)
U.N. diplomat and humanitarian

we move by…

going beyond expectations

going beyond expectations

MEETING EXPECTATIONS IS DOING what's expected.

It's really just our obligation to others.

Unfortunately, in some environments, it's so rare for anyone to meet expectations that doing so is perceived as something special... as if doing the right thing deserved an award and a celebration.

Avoid that kind of thinking. Dismiss mediocrity.

Meeting expectations and doing the right thing are fine first steps, but is it where we want to stop? Think of it this way... is it where we want others to stop when they're doing something for us?

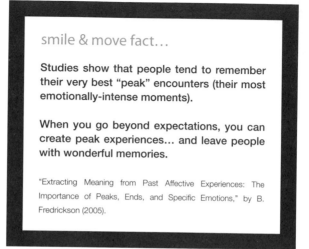

Going beyond expectations is where **wonderful** starts.

Going beyond expectations for others — at work, in our communities, on the field — is how a civil rights movement achieves success, how a Google overtakes a Yahoo!, how an iPod is created and keeps getting better (before we **even ask**).

And we need to remember, sometimes it's the small things that can have a big impact on results.

ISN'T IT TIME TO GET WONDERFUL?

When we save and invest our money, we sometimes put it with individual companies (through mutual funds, stocks, 401(k) plans, etc.). Those companies are made up of people who work to serve a base of customers. Generally speaking, if those people work well — hard and smart — sales and profits will go up, as will the stock price.

If the stock price goes up, our money will grow (our retirement money, college savings money, vacation money, Christmas fund money).

So how hard do you want **those** people to work? As hard as you?

we move by...

having a sense of
of urgency

having a sense of urgency

WHOSE TIME IS THE MOST valuable time on the planet?

Everyone's.

We **all** have to be somewhere, doing something, meeting people, starting this, finishing that.

Every moment counts when **we're** waiting. The same is true when we're serving.

When we're in service-mode, to move (in the Smile & Move sense of the word) is to minimize others' waiting time. It's to predict and pre-sweat the details for those we serve… every time.

MAKE EVERY MOMENT… COUNT.

smile & move fact…

Researchers found that customers who perceived their bank teller as too busy to express emotion — to smile — rated the quality of service very negatively.

"Service with a Smile: Emotional Contagion in the Service Encounter," by S.D. Pugh (2001).

smile & move idea…

Be careful to avoid confusing a sense of urgency with trying to get something off your plate or someone out the door.

Care for someone's time can go beyond just the short-term clock.

Consider instead keeping the concerns of those you serve on your plate with deeper care and follow-through until you're confident they're pleased.

We wanted to work on the balls of our feet...

Yvon Chouinard (1939 -   )
Founder of Patagonia Inc.

we move by…

being resourceful
& resilient

(with no excuses)

being resourceful 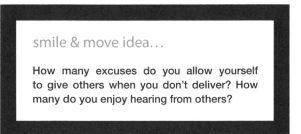 & resilient (with no excuses)

WE WANT SOME THING OR some result.

That's all.

When we visit a store, we want the thing. When we call for help, we want the result.

If we're lucky enough to be in the path of the want, we need to be resourceful in our attempts to make it (whatever **it** is) happen. When we fall short or fail (which we can't always prevent), we need to be resilient.

smile & move idea…

How many excuses do you allow yourself to give others when you don't deliver? How many do you enjoy hearing from others?

Our lack of this resource, the timing of that delivery, the weather, our lack of sleep, tough day, week, month, or year doesn't excuse us from delivering. It just makes it more challenging.

Moving (in the Smile & Move sense) is to move forward — refusing to complain or make excuses. It's remembering that service is about results.

BE HAPPY. DO SOMETHING.

smile & move idea…

How can we help one another create and contribute more value each day?

What if we started by eliminating the TGIF sentiment from our workplaces and schools? What if Fridays became another day of opportunity for service and contribution? What if we pushed it further and stopped perpetuating the idea that Monday is a day of drudgery?

Together, Monday and Friday are 40% of a work week. Imagine the impact if we could get these days back for all those who tend to lose them.

Difficulty is the excuse history **never accepts**.

Edward R. Murrow (1908-1965)
American broadcast journalist

Write it on your heart that **every day is the best day in the year**.

Ralph Waldo Emerson (1803-1882)
Writer and activist

sharing smile&move™

BEFORE PUBLISHING SMILE & MOVE, I shared the idea with many people. Occasionally, I noticed it seemed to rub some the wrong way. (Maybe my delivery was a little less than patient at times, or a little abrasive… I'm working on it.)

Perhaps you'll sometimes have a similar experience.

One way to reopen the lines of communication, I've found, is to talk about how I'm personally challenged with being consistent in my efforts to Smile & Move. Then, I ask the person I'm speaking with when and where they're content with people not smiling and moving for them. Truth is… we all wish that other people behaved this way toward us, and yet sometimes we find it a bit difficult to do so for others.

But that difficulty doesn't really matter, does it?

No matter where we're from, we all know the truth "to treat others as we'd like them to treat us."

SMILE & MOVE.

Generosity is more fun.
That's the key.

Robert Thurman (1941-)
American scholar and Buddhist monk

smile&move™ uncut

I WANT TO GIVE YOU a message.

It's a message I'm sure I was told many times in many ways, but one that I wish I'd embraced much earlier in my life. Because if I had, I'm fairly confident I could have enjoyed much more and contributed in a much larger way.

I wish I'd smiled and moved.

We go to our go-to people because they get the job done. They serve us in a way we can count on more often than the next person (or group, institution, or store).

I wish I were that person more often. I wish I were the go-to person for my particular verse in the world.

It's one of our deepest, most human drives. I want to be needed. You want to be needed. We all want to matter to the world.

After one has discovered what he is called for, he should **set out to do it** with all of the power that he has in his system. Do it as if God almighty ordained you at this particular moment in history to do it.

Martin Luther King Jr. (1929-1968)
Civil rights leader

Smile & Move is a call to go deep within your verse (your work… to the way you contribute) and practice it as Martin Luther King Jr. suggested.

Anything less and we all miss out.

It's about attitude and action. It's about being positive and having a sense of urgency. Being pleased to serve. Having effect.

Mattering to the world, all with a smile.

Not a smile with unchanged eyes… a forced smile. But a smile born of a dramatic, heartfelt understanding that the opportunity to move, to act, to serve someone else in some way is the most wonderful giving-life-meaning chance (yes, chance) that all of us have (although not all of us use).

You're at my service and I'm at yours.

Given a few moments to really consider our personal value proposition in life, how can we come up with it being anything other than service to others?

(Invest those few moments... consider it.)

We want to matter. We want to be relevant.

We also want to be happy. But sometimes we forget where this happiness comes from. And when that happens, we start thinking and acting in ways that are all about what we get rather than what we **give**.

And that attitude keeps us from enjoying so much more.

Big responsibility, big trust, big opportunity, and big money are all earned by creating tremendous value for others. (Certainly there are exceptions, but they're exceptions because they're not the rule.)

If we want to matter and to be happy, if we want more freedom, more flexibility, more responsibility, or more money, we need to give more to those we're supposed to be serving.

We need to get over ourselves.

WE NEED TO SMILE & MOVE.

Work is life, you know, and without it, there's nothing but fear and insecurity.

John Lennon (1940 – 1980)
British musician

about the author

Sam is a co-founder of Give More Media in Richmond, Virginia – a group of people passionately committed to making work better. Since 1998, they've created and published tools, information, and material that help people enjoy more meaning in their work.

Prior to Give More Media, Sam sold products and services in several different industries.

He's also the author of the bestselling book **212° the extra degree**®. He blogs at JustParker.com, occasionally speaks to groups, has a degree in marketing from James Madison University (1987), and does his best to Smile & Move daily.

also by sam

212° the extra degree®

At 211 degrees, water is hot. At 212 degrees, it boils.
And with boiling water, comes steam.
And with steam, **you can power a train**.

Just one extra degree can make all the difference.

212° the extra degree® is an inspiring message with
a singular focus on effort, the most important aspect
of life and work.

The book and material have been purchased and/or
licensed by people at Nike, Wal-Mart, Gap, Verizon,
Hershey, Disney, McDonald's, New York Life, NASCAR,
U.S. Olympic Committee, Marriott, Ernst & Young, Bank
of America, several school systems, and many others.

To enjoy an excerpt from the book and
the 3-minute 212 video, please visit…
www.just212.com

gratitude

So many people have contributed to bringing Smile & Move™ to the world that I feel more like a spokesperson for an important message than the person who gets the byline on the book.

Thank you...

Smovers in the world, for leading by example.

Give More People (today's team and those now giving more elsewhere) for your contributions, patience, candor, and encouragement.

Readers and subscribers of this manifesto, 212, JustSell.com, and my blog.

Angie, Renée, and Bill for helping your Give More People from the outside.

Potential Smovers for inspiring many of the thoughts in the book (you can do it, you want to do it, this is your permission to do it... embrace it... it's more fun).

Jennifer for listening to all of the material – the material that made the book and the material that never made it to the written form. Sam for explaining it as being happy and doing something. Gabriel for being my personal motivational speaker. Sesto for relentlessly smiling and wagging.

Sage and Jordan for pausing to listen at the lemonade stand.

how to use Smile & Move™

Have a copy of Smile & Move™ waiting on your team's desks when they arrive on Monday morning to encourage a new mindset for the coming weeks and months.

Set an expectation of service from day one: give a copy to each new person who joins your organization. Hand one to each new person you're considering hiring, too, so they know the values of the people they may be joining.

License Smile & Move™ material and create a private-label version for your company's team. Include a foreword by your CEO.

Give the book as a gift for graduating high school or college students, sending them into the world with a call to happily serve.

License the logo for use on your organizational materials. Let it serve as a unique reminder to your people.

Reinforce the message all year long with different Smile & Move™ gear (shirts, hats, mugs, etc.).

Make it a theme for an upcoming national, regional, or district event. Use the development material, such as the participants' workbook.

Hand out Smile & Move™ books or mugs at tradeshows to encourage people to engage with you. Let them know you'll Smile & Move™ for them.

Provide the book to your customers, letting them know they can hold you and your team accountable as Smile & Movers.

how to get Smile & Move™

Smile & Move™ is available through Give More Media.

To order the book, training material, and other gear, visit www.GiveMore.com/Smile or call 804-762-4500 ext. 212

For a free printable children's version of Smile & Move™ (for ages 5 – 8), visit www.SmileAndMove.com/Kids

Also available at www.SmileAndMove.com are helpful worksheets for pre-teens, printable mini posters, and computer wallpapers.

Give More. Enjoy More.™

www.LoveYourPeople.com

do something.